CW01512569

Original title:
Echoes of the Mystic Path

Author: Kaido Väinamäe
ISBN HARDBACK: 978-1-80561-371-8
ISBN PAPERBACK: 978-1-80561-932-1

The Songs of the Quiet Glen

In the glen where soft winds sigh,
Whispers dance 'neath the vast blue sky.
Mountains cradle secrets deep,
While the river hums, sweet and steep.

Shadows play on the mossy stone,
Where wildflowers bloom, brightly grown.
Petals flutter with gentle grace,
Nature's heart finds its own place.

Birds weave tunes through rustling leaves,
A melody that never deceives.
Each note sings of tranquil days,
Lost in time, in a peaceful haze.

Stars awaken, the night ignites,
Silver dreams in soft moonlight.
Crickets play their nightly song,
In the glen where hearts belong.

Morning dew brings a fresh new start,
Sunlight glimmers, warms the heart.
In the quiet, life unfolds,
The glen's story gently told.

Whispers in the Twilight Grove

In the hush where shadows blend,
The twilight whispers softly send.
Leaves murmur secrets, lost in flight,
As stars awaken, claiming night.

Moonlight drapes the silent scene,
A silver veil, serene and keen.
Crickets sing their gentle tune,
While echoes lilt 'neath the pale moon.

Branches sway in whispered grace,
Enfolding dreams in their embrace.
A breeze carries tales of old,
Of lovers lost and secrets told.

Footprints tread through grassy lanes,
Where mystery lingers, love refrains.
Each corner turned reveals anew,
Nature's magic casts its view.

So linger here, in twilight's glow,
Where time stands still, and spirits flow.
The whispers weave a soft farewell,
In a grove where peace does dwell.

Shadows Dance on the Silent Trail

Upon the path where shadows play,
Beneath the trees, they sway and sway.
Silence wraps around the night,
As stars ignite with ancient light.

Ghostly figures drift like mist,
In this twilight realm, they coexist.
Whispers float, like leaves that roam,
Along the trail, they find their home.

Echoes of laughter, faint and light,
Merge with the whispers of the night.
Footsteps soft upon the ground,
In this sacred space, peace is found.

The moon hangs low, a watchful eye,
As shadows dance, and moments fly.
In the stillness, dreams take flight,
On the silent trail, through endless night.

So wander deep where spirits weave,
Their stories soft, the heart believes.
In shadows' dance, find your own trail,
Where silence guards and stars prevail.

The Alchemist's Reverie

In a chamber filled with dreams,
The alchemist stirs ancient schemes.
Potions bubble, colors blend,
Each drop a whisper, secrets penned.

Gold and silver luster bright,
Twinkling softly in the night.
Mystic texts laid open wide,
In the heart, where secrets bide.

In this dance of fate and time,
The alchemist weaves thoughts sublime.
Transmuting lead to golden lore,
Unlocking doors forevermore.

With every breath, the cosmos calls,
As knowledge sings through ancient walls.
His hands transform with every thought,
In the cauldron, wisdom caught.

So seek the paths where dreams ignite,
In the realm of shadow and light.
The alchemist's heart is ever free,
In reverie, where magic be.

Veils of Time Unraveled

In the stillness, time entwines,
Veils of memory, soft designs.
Moments flicker, rise and fall,
In whispers heard, we heed the call.

Threads of past and future blend,
In this dance that knows no end.
Twilight lingers, echoes swell,
In the tapestry, stories dwell.

Waves of time, a gentle flow,
Shaping paths we do not know.
In each heartbeat, truths unveil,
Through the fog, our dreams set sail.

Moments stretched like shooting stars,
Guiding lost souls from afar.
The veils that shroud our inner quest,
Reveal the heart, where silence rests.

So wander deep through the unknown,
Embrace the seeds of time you've sown.
For in each breath, a tale unwinds,
In veils of time, our fate aligns.

The Horizon's Embrace

The sun dips low with graceful ease,
A canvas painted, red and gold.
Waves whisper secrets to the breeze,
As night unfolds its stories told.

Eagles soar above the crest,
Their shadows dance on ocean's play.
In tranquil moments we find rest,
As daylight yields to twilight's sway.

The horizon's line, a promise kept,
Where dreams and seas do intertwine.
In every heart, a wish is swept,
To chase the stars, to seek the divine.

Footprints washed away by time,
Yet memories linger of the past.
Each sunset paints a silent rhyme,
A fleeting beauty that will last.

So let us stand at nature's brink,
And feel the warmth of dusk's embrace.
In every heartbeat, pause to think,
Of love and light in this vast space.

Reflections in Starlit Waters

Upon the lake, the stars unite,
Their twinkling dance in silent flow.
The moon, a pearl, casts gentle light,
As whispered dreams begin to grow.

The night reveals what daylight hides,
In every ripple, tales unfold.
Each breeze a story, beckons tides,
As starlit waters gleam like gold.

We sit in wonder, hearts alight,
Their glowing mirrors draw us near.
In soft embrace of velvet night,
Our hopes are whispered, pure and clear.

The world a canvas, ours to paint,
With brushstrokes made of shimmering air.
In stillness, find what hearts might faint,
A tranquil beauty, rich and rare.

Let sorrows drift like gentle leaves,
In twilight's glow, we find our peace.
These starlit waters, where one believes,
In love and dreams, we seek release.

The Journey Beyond the Horizon

Across the sands, the trail unwinds,
With every step, a heartbeat's song.
The horizon calls, the spirit finds,
A path less walked, where we belong.

Mountains rise like ancient guards,
Their peaks adorned with clouds of white.
Through fields of green and scattered shards,
We chase the dawn, embrace the light.

Each moment spent in nature's grace,
Whispers secrets of the old.
In every corner, a hidden place,
Where stories linger, waiting to be told.

The horizon stretches, ever wide,
A promise blooms with every mile.
With open hearts, we must decide,
To journey forth and learn to smile.

So take my hand, let's run away,
Beyond the line where skies ignite.
In every breath, let's seize the day,
And wander freely through the night.

Layers of Light and Shadow

In morning's glow, the shadows play,
A dance of hues, a fleeting dream.
Soft whispers touch the break of day,
As sunlight weaves a golden seam.

With every step, the worlds collide,
A tapestry, of dark and bright.
In every heart, the truths we hide,
Unravel gently in the light.

Evening falls with tender grace,
The colors blend, a soft embrace.
Each layer tells a different tale,
Capturing moments, wide and pale.

So let us wander through this space,
Where shadows linger, truth may rise.
In life's grand weave, we find our place,
In light and dark, our spirits fly.

Here in this realm, we seek, we find,
A balance of the night and day.
In every pulse, our hearts aligned,
In layers rich, we learn to stay.

Beneath the Weeping Willows

In whispers soft, the branches sway,
A gentle breeze, at close of day.
Shadows dance on emerald grass,
Time stands still as moments pass.

The ground is strewn with fallen leaves,
A tapestry of autumn weaves.
Beneath the boughs, a secret sigh,
Emotions flourish, never die.

The sun dips low, the sky ablaze,
In hues of gold, we drift, we gaze.
The world outside fades to a blur,
In nature's arms, our hearts confer.

Daylight wanes, the stars appear,
A quiet peace, the night's sincere.
Beneath the willows, dreams unite,
In the solace of the night.

Together here, we'll weave our tale,
In shadows deep, we will not fail.
Beneath the weeping, life unfolds,
A serenade that never grows old.

A Tapestry Woven in Shadows

In twilight's cloak, we find our place,
The stitches blend in dark embrace.
Threads of silence, colors fade,
A story whispered, softly laid.

The loom of night weaves dreams anew,
In patterns dark, the stars break through.
Each shadow cast an echo's sound,
A harmony in darkness found.

The fabric holds our hopes and fears,
A testament of whispered years.
As shadows shift and tales unfold,
In every fold, a memory bold.

Through layers deep, the heart shall weave,
The tapestry, we won't believe.
For in the night, our spirits blend,
A woven bond that won't unbend.

Together stitched, we face the dawn,
In colors bright, our fears are gone.
A tapestry of light and dark,
In shadows deep, we find our spark.

The Lantern of the Wayfarer

Upon the path, a lantern glows,
Illuminating where one goes.
The flickering light, a guiding star,
Showing the way, near and far.

With every step, shadows retreat,
As dawn approaches on dusty street.
Whispers of wisdom in the night,
The wayfarer's heart, bold and bright.

Worn and weary, yet never lost,
The path ahead, no matter the cost.
Through storms and trials, the lantern shines,
In every struggle, hope entwines.

Each journey taken, a tale begun,
With lantern's light, we greet the sun.
The road ahead, uncertain and wild,
Yet in its warmth, we remain beguiled.

Together we walk, hand in hand,
With lanterns bright, we make our stand.
The wayfarer's heart, forever free,
In light and shadow, we'll always be.

Songs from Beyond the Threshold

In echoes soft, the music swells,
A melody from distant wells.
Songs of old, in whispers flow,
As secrets shared, the spirits know.

Beyond the door, where shadows play,
A symphony of night and day.
Notes entwined in the twilight air,
Each heartbeat sings, a silent prayer.

The threshold crossed, we find our way,
In rhythm lost, yet here we stay.
With every note, the past returns,
In songs of love, the spirit yearns.

Through twilight hues, our voices rise,
A tapestry beneath the skies.
In harmony, our hearts align,
Beyond the threshold, souls entwine.

Together we sing, a sacred rite,
In shadows deep, we seek the light.
With every chord, our hearts will sway,
In songs that guide us through the fray.

The Whispering Stones of Eldoria

In the glen where shadows play,
The stones sing secrets of old.
Whispers of time float gently by,
Guarded tales in silence told.

Moss-covered wisdom lingers near,
Echoes of laughter, soft as dew.
Each pebble holds a memory,
Of worlds where dreams once flew.

Underneath the twilight's glow,
The ancient voices intertwine.
Each note a thread in fate's design,
Binding hearts to the divine.

As the stars in the night unfold,
The winds carry voices anew.
Eldoria whispers, bold and bright,
Embracing all that's tried and true.

Haunts of the Celestial Dreamers

In the realms where starlight weaves,
The dreamers dance on silver beams.
With cosmic hearts, they rise and drift,
Tales unfolding in hidden dreams.

Each sigh a spark in skies so deep,
Galaxies swirl, they weave their art.
In shadows cast by shooting stars,
Lies a melody of the heart.

Celestial whispers guide their paths,
To lands of wonder, vast and grand.
Through nebulas, they float and glide,
With hopes and wishes in their hands.

In twilight's realm, they find their peace,
While the universe softly sings.
The haunts of dreamers, ever bright,
In a timeless dance, they take to wings.

The Tranquil Pulse of Nature's Heart

Beneath the canopy of green,
A heartbeat echoes, pure and clear.
Whispers of leaves in gentle breeze,
Nature's song, for all to hear.

Rivers flow with steadfast grace,
Reflecting sunlight's playful dance.
Mountains stand in quiet pride,
Guardians of the earth's romance.

Each flower blooms in vibrant hues,
A tapestry of life displayed.
In every petal lies a dream,
Of nature's love and joy portrayed.

As evening falls with softest sighs,
The stars awaken one by one.
Nature's pulse, a soothing balm,
Cradles the world 'neath moon and sun.

Pathways through the Mystical Fog

In the mist where shadows blend,
Whispers lead to paths unknown.
Step by step, the journey calls,
Guiding hearts to places grown.

Veils of fog like dreams obscure,
As secrets dance in twilight's hue.
Each turn unveils a mystery,
A world reborn, a vision new.

The air is thick with magic's breath,
A melody of soft delight.
With every footfall, courage stirs,
To chase the dawn, to seek the light.

Through tangled woods and glimmering streams,
Adventures wait in every sigh.
The pathways twist, yet hearts remain,
Bound by dreams that never die.

Cabal of the Crystal Dawn

In dawn's embrace, secrets unfold,
Whispers of dreams in colors bold.
Gathered shadows on the rise,
Eyes aglow with morning's guise.

Crystals gleam in morning's light,
Casting spells to start the fight.
With every breath, a pact is sealed,
Revealing truths once concealed.

Through veils of mist, they dance and sway,
Guiding fortunes lost in gray.
A silent pact, the dawn awakes,
Echoes of fate in crystal lakes.

In the circle, they find their way,
Energies blend in bright array.
The power lies in shared intent,
As heartbeats quicken, dark is spent.

So grasp the dawn, hold it tight,
In the cabal, find your light.
Together in the morning glow,
Awaken dreams and let them flow.

Illusions of the Journeying Mind

Through winding paths, the shadows creep,
Whispers linger, secrets deep.
Images dance on fleeting thought,
In the maze, what have we sought?

Mirrors reflect a hidden guise,
Truths cloaked in subtle lies.
Each step taken, reality bends,
A cycle that never ends.

Clouds of doubt, they shape the skies,
Vision blurred by fleeting highs.
Yet in the heart, a spark ignites,
Guiding souls through haunting nights.

Veils of color hide the pain,
Journey marked by joy and strain.
With every twist, a lesson learned,
Through fire and doubt, spirits burned.

So dare to travel, break the chain,
For in the struggle lies the gain.
Through illusions, find your way,
In the mind, dreams dance and play.

Serene Spheres of Serendipity

In the calm of twilight's hue,
Spheres of wonder, bright and new.
Moment's grace, a gentle glide,
In stillness, magic will abide.

Each breath a gift, a treasure rare,
Lost in time, the world laid bare.
Harmony sings in whispered tones,
In the silence, peace is sown.

Stars align in perfect form,
Guiding hearts to weather storms.
Through chance encounters, joy is found,
In endless cycles, love unbound.

Embrace the light, let shadows fade,
Serendipity's dance, a serenade.
In every glimmer, hope resides,
Boundless wonders in life's tides.

Thus, wander forth with open eyes,
In serene spheres, the spirit flies.
For in each moment, truth can gleam,
Life unfolds as a wondrous dream.

The Alluring Shadows of the Night Garden

In gardens where the moonlight weaves,
Alluring shadows hum like leaves.
Petals whisper secrets low,
In the night, enchantments grow.

Winding paths in velvet dark,
Each turn hides a whispered spark.
Gentle sighs in fragrant air,
With every step, a call laid bare.

Beneath the stars, the heart takes flight,
Dancing shadows, pure delight.
In the hush of twilight's song,
Night's embrace where we belong.

Glistening dew on tender skin,
In this space, new dreams begin.
Linger here, let time slip by,
In night's garden, find the sky.

So let the shadows guide your heart,
In their whispers, play your part.
For in the night's embrace, you'll find,
The allure of the garden kind.

Guardians of the Sacred Path

In whispers low, they stand and wait,
With watchful eyes to guard your fate.
Beneath the moon, through timbered glade,
They keep the secrets, softly laid.

The winds do speak, their voices clear,
With tales of ages long since near.
Each step you take, a dance with fate,
Guardians follow, patient, straight.

The shadows weave their mystic thread,
In every prayer, a word unsaid.
They guide the lost, the weary soul,
To find the light and feel made whole.

Through trials deep, in silence swell,
They weave the dreams, the sacred well.
With courage high, and spirits bright,
The path unfolds, in soft moonlight.

So heed the call, let heart be free,
For guardians walk in mystery.
In sacred paths, your truth align,
With nature's breath, your spirit shine.

The Unseen Bridges of the Soul

Beneath the surface, whispers flow,
Connections deep that we may know.
An unseen bridge, a thread so fine,
Links hearts and minds in pure design.

In shadows cast, they intertwine,
With every laugh, with every sign.
Though miles apart, they bind as one,
In silent dance 'neath shadows spun.

The language shared, a glance, a sigh,
In dreams we meet, we learn to fly.
The heartbeats sync, a rhythm true,
In time's embrace, a bond renew.

Through storms that rage, through nights so long,
These bridges form our spirits strong.
In unity, we rise and fall,
Together woven, answering the call.

So trust the path, though hard to see,
These bridges guide our destiny.
With every step, we reach the goal,
The unseen bridges of the soul.

Murmurs of the Sacred Well

In twilight's hush, the waters gleam,
A sacred well, a whispered dream.
With every drop, a secret shared,
Of hopes and fears, the heart laid bare.

The echoes call, from depths unknown,
They speak of past, and seeds long sown.
In silence deep, the truths arise,
Like gentle waves, beneath the skies.

The liquid thoughts, they swirl and flow,
A mirror held to what we know.
In crystal depths, reflections glow,
As wisdom drips, so sweet and slow.

Through time's embrace, the well will wait,
For souls to seek, and contemplate.
In murmurs soft, the stories swell,
Unraveling the sacred well.

So lean in close, and hear the sound,
Of tales that wait, in silence found.
With every drop, a journey's tell,
As life unfolds, within the well.

Crystalline Visions in the Fog

In shrouded mist, where shadows play,
The world transformed, in hues of gray.
Crystalline sights break through the haze,
Revealing wonders in strange ways.

A glimmer bright, a fleeting glance,
In fractured light, we find our chance.
Each vision bold, a whisper clear,
Awakens dreams that disappear.

As fog retreat, horizons show,
The paths we take, where we must go.
In clarity, the heart does sing,
Of hopes reborn, of truths we bring.

Through veils of time, in morning's grace,
The crystalline forms begin to chase.
In every step, a choice revealed,
In fog's embrace, our fate unsealed.

So trust the light that breaks the mist,
For in each vision, love exists.
Embrace the fog, let worries thaw,
In crystalline visions, find the awe.

Beneath the Canopy of Celestial Beings

Stars whisper softly in night's embrace,
Moonlight glimmers on leaves with grace.
Dreams swirl gently in twilight's glow,
Nature's secrets in silence flow.

A dance of shadows beneath the skies,
Mysteries unfold as the night sighs.
In the stillness, old stories wake,
From the depths of time, paths we take.

Fern fronds beckon, reaching high,
To greet the constellations up in the sky.
With every rustle, the tales are spun,
Of battles fought and glories won.

Awakened spirits, watchful and wise,
Guardians of dreams beneath the night skies.
In this haven, our hearts can roam,
Beneath the canopy, we find our home.

The Enigmatic Dance of Fireflies

In the glade, the fireflies play,
Twinkling softly, fading away.
They flicker like stars caught in flight,
Dancing magic in the velvet night.

Whispers of secrets in the dusk air,
A symphony glows with a gentle flare.
In their glow, a moment suspended,
Capturing dreams as the night intended.

As shadows lengthen, they weave and spin,
Guiding lost souls beneath their din.
The world transforms in their delicate light,
A fleeting enchantment before the dawn's sight.

In this ballet, we find our delight,
Fleeting wonders that brighten the night.
Their dance a reminder, ephemeral and bright,
Of beauty residing in the heart of night.

Mythos of the Twilit Realm

In the twilight hour, where secrets lie,
A realm awakens under the sky.
Hushed tones weave the tales once told,
Of battles fierce and hearts bold.

Frosted whispers from shadows emerge,
A mystery deep in twilight's surge.
Wanderers pause to heed the call,
Of ancients lingering amidst it all.

Stars align, their stories collide,
In this liminal zone, worlds abide.
Between light and shadow, echoes persist,
Of forgotten lore and enchanting mist.

In every breath, the night unfolds,
A tapestry rich of adventures bold.
Here lies the essence of fate entwined,
A mythos waiting for hearts to find.

A Journey Guided by Starlight

In the hush of night, we set our course,
With starlight's glow, a guiding force.
Celestial maps over oceans wide,
Lead us onward with each tide.

Footsteps light on the dewy grass,
Following constellations as they pass.
Each twinkle whispers of places unknown,
Inviting hearts to venture alone.

Through valleys deep and mountains steep,
We capture wonders, memories to keep.
The sky, a canvas where dreams take flight,
In every shimmer, hope ignites.

So let us roam beneath the vast dome,
With starlight as our guide, we feel at home.
A journey unfolds with each breath we take,
Under the watchful eyes, we embrace the awake.

Whispers of Forgotten Trails

In the woods where shadows lie,
Footsteps echo, soft and shy.
Leaves rustle with the tales they keep,
Ancient secrets, lost in sleep.

Through the bramble, echoes call,
Memories dance, the night enthralls.
Moonlight weaves a silver thread,
Winding paths where dreams have fled.

By the stream, a gentle sigh,
Whispering tales as time slips by.
Every stone holds a story told,
In the breeze, their voices bold.

Roots entangle, years unfold,
Nature whispers, clear yet old.
Each turn reveals what once was near,
Lost in time, yet always here.

In the dusk, the shadows gleam,
Guiding lost souls in a dream.
Footsteps fade as night prevails,
In whispers soft, forgotten trails.

Shadows of the Celestial Journey

Stars ignite the velvet sky,
Drawing dreams that dare to fly.
Planets spin in silent grace,
Light years pass in endless space.

Comets trace a blazing arc,
Whispers carried through the dark.
Galaxies spin in cosmic dance,
Eternal waltz of circumstance.

Nebulae bloom with colors bold,
Stories of the cosmos told.
In their heart, the spark of life,
Endless wonders, joy and strife.

Through the void, a path unfolds,
In each heartbeat, universe holds.
Traveling on the stardust trail,
Guided by the cosmic sail.

Celestial shadows softly call,
In their embrace, we rise and fall.
Boundless skies, our spirits soar,
Journey bright, forevermore.

The Serpent's Silent Song

In the forest where shadows creep,
The serpent stirs from ancient sleep.
Silent coils in emerald hue,
Whispers secrets only few.

Through the grass, a gentle sway,
Nature hums its soft ballet.
Eyes aglow with mystic gleam,
Crafting tales that twist and seam.

Beneath the moon's embracing light,
The serpent dances through the night.
Each scale glistens, stories writ,
In the silence, shadows sit.

Nature's rhythm pulses deep,
In the stillness, secrets seep.
A silent song, the heartbeats share,
The serpent's whisper fills the air.

Through the dusk, a mystic throng,
Echoes of the silent song.
In the forest, time stands still,
As the serpent weaves its will.

Reflections in the Moonlit Mist

On the lake, the moonlight spills,
Casting dreams on gentle hills.
Mirror surfaces, calm and bright,
Whispers wrapped in silver light.

In the mist, a world unfolds,
Stories woven, softly told.
Each ripple holds a fleeting gaze,
Reflections dance in twilight haze.

By the shore, the nightingale sings,
A serenade on whispered wings.
Melodies weave through fragrant air,
In the stillness, hearts laid bare.

Footsteps trace the path of dreams,
Lost in thought, light softly gleams.
Beneath the stars, a quiet wish,
In the moonlit mist, hearts swish.

Time meanders, soft and slow,
With every breath, the whispers flow.
In the night's embrace, we find,
Moonlit tales with peace entwined.

Musings in the Celestial Mist

Stars whisper secrets, soft and bright,
Glowing in silence, a wondrous sight.
Night wraps the world in a velvet shroud,
Dreams take flight, beneath sky unbowed.

Clouds drift like thoughts, soft and unclear,
Echoes of wishes, drawing us near.
Galaxies dance in a cosmic waltz,
Lost in the magic, we halt at the pulse.

Comets weave tales, a fleeting glance,
Life's mysteries beckon, as if to dance.
Planets align, ancient paths known,
In the mist of the heavens, we're never alone.

Whispers of stardust, linger and call,
Holding our hopes, in the cosmic sprawl.
Infinitesimal wonders, vast and profound,
In the celestial mist, our souls are unbound.

As night turns to dawn, the stars fade away,
Yet their light in our hearts will forever stay.
Musing on all that the night has bestowed,
In the quiet of morning, we carry the load.

The Altar of Wandering Souls

In the shadows flicker, candles burn low,
Silent prayers linger, in whispers they flow.
Candor of spirits, lost and confined,
Gathered together, in heart and in mind.

The altar stands firm, with promises made,
Each token laid gently, a love never frayed.
Echoes of longing, a soft serenade,
Binding the past with the choices we've made.

Wandering souls with their tales intertwined,
Finding the solace that life left behind.
In every tear shed, in every embrace,
We honor the memories, time cannot erase.

Light flickers softly, a dance in the air,
Waves of compassion, we offer our care.
In this sacred space, we forge what we share,
The altar of wandering, a love laid bare.

Through darkened valleys and brighter skies,
We keep our hearts open, as the spirit flies.
In the shadows of dreams, we always remain,
At the altar of souls, we'll gather again.

Reflections in a Still Pool

Glimmers of sunlight drop softly down,
Kissing the water, a silken crown.
Mirrors of moments, gently unfold,
In the stillness, secrets are told.

Ripples of laughter, echo in time,
Soft whispers linger, a rhythmic chime.
Framed by the willows, and petals so sweet,
Nature's embrace, where our hearts meet.

Clouds drift above, casting shadows wide,
In the still pool's gaze, where we confide.
Every reflection a glimpse of the past,
A dance with the memories, meant to last.

Stillness surrounds as the world moves fast,
We find our moments, in reflections cast.
Beneath the green willows, our thoughts intertwine,
In the quiet of water, our souls align.

With each passing breeze, the layers peel back,
Revealing the essence that hides in the black.
In the still pool's heart, we dive and we play,
Finding ourselves in the echoes of day.

Tread Softly Through the Veil

In twilight's embrace, shadows softly dance,
Treading gently, in a veiled romance.
Whispers of secrets float on the air,
Hidden among dreams, that linger with care.

Moonbeams like fingers caress the night,
Calling us softly to follow their light.
The veil between worlds, so thin and so fine,
Guiding our hearts like a celestial sign.

Echoes of laughter, entwined with the breeze,
Carrying murmurs of ancient trees.
In this sacred hour, where magic prevails,
We find our way through the soft, silken trails.

With patience we wander, through shadows' soft weave,
Unraveling stories, we learn to believe.
In the stillness we seek, the truth will unveil,
As we tread softly, through the thin, mystic veil.

A journey of wonder, of love and of light,
Embracing the whispers that beckon the night.
In the heart of the mystery, we will not fail,
Treading together, through the veil, we will sail.

Celestial Paint on the Canvas of Night

Stars twinkle like diamonds, bright,
The moon spills silver on the earth,
Whispers of cosmos take flight,
In darkness, we find rebirth.

Nebulas dance in vibrant hues,
Galaxies swirl in cosmic grace,
Each stroke of light a muse,
Nature's wonder, time's embrace.

Comets blaze with fiery trails,
Echoes of a million tales,
In the vastness, our hearts align,
Boundless dreams in starry design.

Planets spin in silent song,
Music of the spheres unfolds,
Guided by the night so long,
In the universe, we behold.

As dawn approaches, shadows fade,
Yet the memories linger bright,
Celestial paint will never jade,
Illuminated by the night.

Fragmented Dreams of a Wanderer

Footsteps echo on distant trails,
Whispers of where the heart once strayed,
Each journey brings both fears and gales,
In fragmented dreams, we are swayed.

Mountains rise, shadows conceal,
Rivers carve paths through ancient stone,
What secrets does the night reveal?
The wanderer's spirit, never alone.

Through fields of wildflowers, I roam,
Seeking a place to call my own,
But shadows whisper, calling me home,
In a world where the heart has grown.

Stars above guide my weary way,
Each spark a promise, bright and rare,
With every night, the dreams replay,
Of distant lands, I long to share.

Yet in the silence, hope resides,
For every wanderer finds their thread,
And in the heart, a truth abides,
That even lost, we forge ahead.

The Silence Between the Stars

In the void where silence reigns,
Echoes of thoughts drift like dust,
Whispers of light, memories of pains,
A tapestry woven in trust.

Stars shimmer in the vast expanse,
Guardians of secrets buried deep,
In their glow, we find a chance,
To discover dreams that softly sleep.

Between the twinkles, stories dwell,
Silent songs of fate and time,
In their beauty, we hear the swell,
Of life's pulse, a rhythmic rhyme.

Galaxies spin, in quietude,
Embracing the stillness of night,
In postures of grace, a interlude,
Where darkness and brilliance unite.

Within this silence, hearts can soar,
Floating on stardust, they roam free,
For in the quiet, we explore,
The cosmos of possibility.

When the Forest Sings

Beneath the canopy, whispers flow,
Leaves rustle with secrets untold,
In the heart of the trees, a glow,
Life and magic, vibrant and bold.

Roots entwined in ancient lore,
Each branch a verse in nature's rhyme,
In harmony, we find much more,
Than the ticking of the hands of time.

Birdsong dances through the air,
Notes rising like the morning sun,
In this cradle, joy and care,
Nature's symphony has begun.

Mossy carpets beneath our feet,
Echoes of laughter, murmurs of peace,
As creatures join in, hearts skip a beat,
In the forest, all worries cease.

When twilight falls, the stars will gleam,
A hush descends, and silence sings,
In the stillness, we weave a dream,
With the forest, our hearts take wings.

A Tapestry of Twilight Hues

The sky unfolds in shades of pink,
Where whispers of the night begin to sink.
Soft shadows dance on the velvet ground,
In this fleeting moment, peace is found.

Stars emerge with a gentle glow,
As twilight paints a world so slow.
The breeze carries secrets through the trees,
While dreams awaken on the evening's knees.

Crickets serenade the moonlit air,
Each note a promise, a tender care.
A brush of twilight, a splash of grace,
In the horizon's embrace, the day leaves trace.

Colors mingle, a brushstroke of fate,
As the universe whispers, it's not too late.
To find the beauty in shades that blend,
In this tapestry, the night transcends.

In stillness, life in hues remains,
A quiet moment behind the stains.
Beneath the stars, we lose our way,
In the tapestry of twilight, dreams sway.

The Language of Ancient Stones

In the silence of the stones, they speak,
Of time long gone and futures bleak.
Marks of history, weathered and worn,
In each crack, a tale is born.

Whispers of empires that once stood tall,
Echo in shadows, memories call.
The moss gathers secrets of ages past,
In a language of silence, forever vast.

From crumbled walls, the voices rise,
A symphony woven beneath the skies.
Each stone a witness to laughter and tears,
Telling of joys and burying fears.

The ruins hold stories that never fade,
In the heart of the earth, the past is laid.
With every touch, a connection grows,
In the stillness of time, eternity flows.

In the language of stones, we find our place,
A reminder of life's tender grace.
Listen closely, let the silence embrace,
For ancient stones hold time's warm trace.

Reverberations in the Stillness

In the stillness, echoes softly play,
Whispers of thoughts that drift away.
Between the silence, a pulse can be felt,
In the warmth of moments, emotions melt.

The heartbeats linger, a measured sound,
In quiet corners, where dreams are found.
Each breath a note in the song of the night,
Guiding the weary back to light.

Time stretches thin, a gossamer thread,
Carrying wishes that linger, unsaid.
Reverberations of laughter and sighs,
In the calm of the evening, where stillness lies.

We dance in shadows, unvoiced delight,
In the palette of silence, our souls take flight.
Each moment captured, like fireflies glow,
In reverberations, our true selves show.

In the stillness we cherish, we find our way,
Navigating paths that dreams convey.
The echoes of life, both tender and bold,
In the fabric of silence, our stories unfold.

The Enigma of the Wandering Star

A star drifts softly across the sky,
Carrying secrets like a whispered sigh.
It wanders through night, a cosmic dance,
In its flicker, we find a chance.

It twinkles with meaning, heavy yet light,
A guide for the lost in the velvet night.
Each twirl and twist, a riddle to see,
In the enigma of dreams, possibility.

Across the heavens, it journeys afar,
With tales of wonder, the wandering star.
Forever it travels, never confined,
A beacon for souls that seek and find.

In its gleam, we glimpse our fate,
A reminder that dreams are never late.
With every blink, a wish is spun,
In the tapestry of time, we are one.

Oh, wandering star, guide us tonight,
Through darkness and shadows, into the light.
A dance with the cosmos, a promise to keep,
In the enigma of wonder, our dreams take leap.

Threads of Destiny in the Breeze

Whispers weave through the gentle air,
Carrying dreams with utmost care.
Fleeting moments, like petals fall,
Each a story, each a call.

In the twilight, shadows blend,
Threads of fate on which we depend.
Nature's hand in subtle grace,
Guiding us to our rightful place.

Under skies that shift and dance,
Every heartbeat, a second chance.
Through the valleys, over hills,
Love's embrace, the spirit thrills.

Entwined paths in the golden light,
Dreams take flight, hearts ignite.
In the silence, truth unfolds,
Threads of destiny, a tale retold.

As day meets night in soft retreat,
We find the rhythm, the pulse, the beat.
In every sigh, a journey new,
Threads of destiny guide us through.

The Dance of Light and Shadow

In the dawn, where shadows play,
Light weaves colors in bright array.
Moments flicker, a canvas clear,
Dance of contrasts, drawing near.

Under stars that wink and gleam,
Night whispers secrets, soft as dreams.
A ballet spun in moonlit grace,
Harmony found in this sacred space.

Colors blend in twilight's embrace,
Light and shadow share their place.
Every flicker tells a tale,
In their union, fears grow pale.

As dusk unfolds its velvet shroud,
Life rebels against the crowd.
In fleeting moments of surprise,
We catch a glimpse, the world arises.

With every dawn, shadows retreat,
Yet in their dance, we feel complete.
Light ignites, shadows confess,
In their company, we find our rest.

Sages Beneath the Evergreen

Ancient trees with wisdom grand,
Sages gather, hand in hand.
Whispers echo through the leaves,
Time, they say, forever weaves.

Gentle breezes carry tales,
Of distant lands and bustling trails.
In the shade, beneath the pine,
Thoughts converge, and souls entwine.

Beneath the boughs, we find reprieve,
Lessons learned, and dreams believe.
Nature's pulse, the heartbeat strong,
Guiding us where we belong.

In silence shared, the heart beats true,
Sages speak, so wise and new.
With every breeze, a truth bestowed,
In the evergreen, wisdom flowed.

As time moves on and seasons change,
We gather 'round, our thoughts arranged.
In nature's arms, we come alive,
Beneath the trees, our spirits thrive.

The Winding Stream's Serenade

A stream flows softly, singing low,
In its current, tales bestow.
Ripples laugh as they leap and swirl,
Drawing whispers from the world.

Through the meadow, over stones,
The water hums, and softly moans.
Every twist, a secret shared,
Flowing freely, hearts ensnared.

Beneath the bridges worn and gray,
Journeys mark the waterway.
With every bend, a memory,
In the stream's embrace, we see.

Nature's voice in gentle glide,
Carries hope on every tide.
In its song, we find our way,
Winding paths where dreams can play.

As moonlight dances on the crest,
We find the peace, the heart's sweet rest.
In the stream's serenade so sweet,
Life flows on, our souls complete.

The Path of Silent Encounters

In shadows deep, we walk alone,
Whispers echo, secrets sown.
A gentle glance, a fleeting smile,
We share a bond, though just a while.

Beneath the stars, our spirits meet,
Silent words, no need for speech.
Hearts entwined in quiet grace,
Moments linger, time can't erase.

Through twilight paths, we roam unbound,
In every silence, love is found.
Nature holds our dreams so near,
Each heartbeat is a truth we hear.

The night unfolds its velvet veil,
In stillness, we begin to sail.
With every step, our souls align,
In this embrace, the world is fine.

Heartbeats in the Cosmic Symphony

In the hush of night, stars ignite,
Heartbeat echoes, pure delight.
Melodies of the universe,
Lift our spirits, break the curse.

Every pulse is a grand design,
Harmony in space and time.
Planets dance in radiant bliss,
In each note, a cosmic kiss.

Galaxies whisper ancient tunes,
Drawing us to their vibrant moons.
In every breath, a story spins,
Through the cosmos, our journey begins.

We rise and fall, in love's embrace,
Lost in the rhythm of this space.
With heartbeats strong, we sway and glide,
In the symphony, side by side.

The Unopened Book of Dreams

Tucked away on a dusty shelf,
Whispers of worlds, lost to self.
Pages waiting, untouched by time,
In each chapter, a hidden rhyme.

Worn edges tell tales untold,
Ventures waiting, brave and bold.
With every turn, a new refrain,
Unlock the doors, embrace the gain.

Nighttime secrets softly plead,
Stories planted like a seed.
In your hands, the key is bright,
Illuminate the dawn with light.

Dreams await, don't hesitate,
In every line, we navigate.
With open heart, begin to see,
In this book, find your decree.

A Tidal Breeze of Celestial Musings

Upon the shore, the waves do sigh,
A gentle breeze, the night draws nigh.
With every crest, thoughts drift away,
In the twilight, we wish to stay.

Celestial musings, soft and sweet,
Where land and sky in stillness meet.
The moonlight dances on the sea,
In its glow, we find our glee.

Casting dreams upon the tide,
In the current, we confide.
Each heartbeat flows, a whisper shared,
In this moment, we are bared.

Through the night, we softly muse,
In the silence, we refuse.
Let the tide guide our souls anew,
In this journey, me and you.

Drifting Clouds of Forgotten Yesterdays

Soft whispers ride the gentle breeze,
Echoes of laughter through the trees.
Memories linger like fading light,
Chasing the dawn, escaping the night.

Lost moments drift on silken threads,
Dreams entwined where the silence spreads.
Time weaves tales of joy and sorrow,
Bathed in the glow of a bright tomorrow.

Faces and places, they come and go,
In waves of remembrance, ebb and flow.
Clouds shift softly, painting the sky,
As we chase tales that never say goodbye.

Yearning hearts seek what once was near,
Wrapped in the magic of yesteryear.
Beneath the skies where memories roam,
We find solace, we find our home.

So let the clouds drift, let them play,
In the canvas of life, they guide the way.
Painting our stories in shades of grey,
Drifting clouds of forgotten yesterdays.

The Call of the Wind's Embrace

In the stillness, a whisper calls,
Through the valley, where silence falls.
A gentle breath that beckons me near,
Promising tales only the wind can hear.

With every gust, a secret shared,
The rustling leaves, a world declared.
Dancing shadows in a twilight glow,
The call of the wind, an endless flow.

Over mountains, through ancient trees,
It carries stories of distant seas.
Embracing the moments, fleeting and bright,
The wind holds dreams in the soft moonlight.

When I close my eyes, I hear its song,
A melody sweet, where I belong.
Guiding my heart on a path unknown,
In the wind's embrace, I've found my home.

Ceaseless whispers, forever roam,
In every breeze, I reclaim my own.
For in the currents, my spirit flies,
The call of the wind beneath open skies.

The Lorekeepers of Time's Gaze

Ancient stones whisper through the years,
Guardians of moments, joy and fears.
Each crack a tale, each grain a song,
In their silence, we all belong.

Through changing ages, they stand tall,
In twilight shadows, they hear the call.
The lorekeepers watch as life unfolds,
Their secrets wrapped in the tales they hold.

Time weaves magic with every breath,
In the dance of life, we encounter death.
Yet within the cycles, hope still thrives,
In the heart of the earth, every spirit derives.

With every sunrise, the past recalls,
Echoes of laughter, the heart enthralls.
The stories entwined in time's own thread,
In the lorekeepers' gaze, we are led.

As seasons shift and ages align,
We find our roots in their divine.
For in the fabric of life's embrace,
The lorekeepers dwell in time's steadfast grace.

When Shadows Breathe in Color

In twilight hours, shadows awaken,
With hues of dreams, their forms unshaken.
As daylight fades, the colors blend,
Whispers of night, where mysteries send.

From silhouettes, stories arise,
Painted in tones of darkened skies.
A dance of light in the fading glow,
When shadows breathe, the wonders flow.

Crimson and gold, a canvas unfurls,
In the depth of dusk, a world twirls.
Shadows embrace the twilight's kiss,
In every corner, there lies bliss.

Voices of night in a vivid dream,
Streaming through starlight, they softly gleam.
The heartbeat of dusk in a vibrant swirl,
When shadows breathe, the night unfurls.

So let us wander where colors blend,
In the breaths of shadows, our hearts ascend.
For in this realm, both wild and free,
When shadows breathe, we come to see.

Secrets in the Rustling Leaves

Whispers dance in autumn's breath,
Golden hues of life's short quest.
Each leaf a story weaves and weaves,
Secrets hidden in rustling leaves.

Crisp mornings cradle quiet thoughts,
Nature's wisdom gently taught.
In shadows soft, the echoes tease,
Unlocking whispers in the breeze.

Underneath the boughs we find,
A tapestry that nature's lined.
Comfort found in swaying trees,
Healing promises in the leaves.

A soft rustle, a gentle sigh,
Memories linger, drifting by.
In every crack and creak, it weaves,
Our secret hopes among the leaves.

The Veil Between Worlds

A shimmer glows in twilight's grace,
A passage veiled, a hidden space.
Where whispers tread on silvered ground,
And echoes of the lost are found.

Between the stars, the shadows breathe,
Memories linger, hearts believe.
The dance of time, a mysterious art,
Binding realms, yet keeping apart.

In twilight's mist, the spirits meet,
With every heartbeat, they entreat.
A gentle pull, a timeless thread,
Weaving destinies of the dead.

Through swirling fog, the truth unveils,
In silence deep, the spirit trails.
A tapestry of hopes and fears,
The veil between us thins with tears.

In Search of the Celestial Map

Starry nights call out our dreams,
Guiding seekers with silver beams.
Constellations carved in the sky,
Whispering answers as worlds pass by.

A compass forged from longing hearts,
Leading us where the starlight starts.
With every twinkle, secrets bloom,
In the vastness, we find our room.

Each ancient star a story's thread,
From cosmic fires to realms we've tread.
In search of paths that futures show,
The map unfolds as spirits grow.

In cosmic dance, we find our place,
Guided by light in soft embrace.
With every pulse, our spirits clap,
As we traverse the celestial map.

The Timeless Chronicle of Echoing Voices

In deep caverns of the past,
Echoes linger, shadows cast.
Whispers weave through ages lost,
Chronicles spoken, no matter the cost.

Voices brush against the soul,
Tales of sorrow, joy, and whole.
In the silence, echoes swell,
Remnants of stories they must tell.

Each heartbeat carries tales of old,
In the fabric of life, the truth unfolds.
A timeless chorus calls our name,
Awakening spirits, fanning the flame.

From ancient stones to hearts ablaze,
We listen close to the mystic haze.
In every echo, wisdom grows,
The timeless chronicle softly flows.

Labyrinths of Time and Memory

In shadows deep, the echoes play,
Winding paths where lost dreams sway.
Each corner turned, a whisper found,
In tangled thoughts, our hearts unbound.

Fleeting moments, grain of sand,
Carved in silence, ever grand.
Memories dance in twilight's glow,
A labyrinth where we dare not go.

Faces fading, stories blend,
The forest speaks of paths we bend.
Time entwined, a needle's thread,
In morning's light, the past is fed.

Through winding ways, we search in vain,
Seeking solace in joy and pain.
The echoes call, we heed their plea,
In this maze, we long to be free.

Yet every turn brings forth a choice,
Whispers linger, a haunting voice.
In the heart of time, shadows loom,
With every step, we face our doom.

Spirits in the Silent Grove

Beneath the boughs, where secrets lie,
Gentle murmurs catch the sky.
In twilight's hush, the spirits roam,
A hidden world, a whispered home.

Among the leaves, a soft refrain,
Echoes linger of love and pain.
They weave through branches, soft and light,
Dancing shadows in fading night.

Ethereal dreams in the cooling air,
The scent of magic, alive and rare.
Mirth and sorrow blend as one,
In silent groves where time is spun.

Ghostly laughter fills the night,
In the quiet, a fleeting sight.
Emerging from the twilight haze,
Spirits whisper in forgotten ways.

So linger here, if you dare,
For in stillness, no soul can spare.
Embrace the still, let shadows creep,
In the grove where silence weeps.

Footprints on the Starlit Sands

Under the stars, the night unfolds,
Whispers of tales that time holds.
Footprints traced in silver grains,
Stories linger, love remains.

Waves caress, a soothing song,
Drawn to shores where we belong.
Every step, a wish, a dream,
In moonlight's glow, we softly gleam.

Barefoot wanderers find their way,
Lost in night, come what may.
Kissed by breezes, hearts in flight,
Painting memories in soft moonlight.

The ocean sighs, a tranquil sound,
With every step, the world unbound.
Light as feathers, soft as sighs,
We trace our path beneath the skies.

These footprints fade with morning's rise,
Yet in our hearts, the starlight lies.
For every grain of sand we tread,
Is a memory of love we bled.

The Call of the Hidden Vale

In valleys lush, where spirits dwell,
A secret call, a sacred bell.
Winds whisper through the ancient trees,
Inviting souls to come with ease.

Golden rays spill through the leaves,
Where every breath the heart believes.
In quiet corners, echoes play,
The hidden vale beckons, come away.

Rivers sing of tales untold,
As leaves of autumn blush to gold.
In still waters, reflections dance,
A mystic realm, a fleeting chance.

With every step, the path unveils,
Stories woven in nature's gales.
In the vale, our spirits soar,
Eternal whispers, longing for more.

So heed the call of distant light,
In the hidden vale, all feels right.
Embrace the journey, feel the grace,
In nature's heart, we find our place.

Chasing the Horizon's Secrets

Beyond the hills the sun does rise,
A canvas painted with orange skies.
Waves of light in gentle flow,
Secrets whispering, tales of glow.

With every step, the path unfolds,
A journey where adventure molds.
Footprints marked in golden sand,
Chasing dreams, a future planned.

The colors melt, a radiant hue,
A promise made, a heart so true.
Each shadow casts a fleeting glance,
Inviting all to join the dance.

The horizon beckons, calls my name,
A quest ignited, burning flame.
Through distant lands, I'll roam in peace,
Seeking treasures that never cease.

In twilight's arms, the stars align,
A boundless sky, a cosmic sign.
Together we'll unveil the night,
Chasing secrets 'til morning light.

Beneath the Veil of Dreams

In the silence where shadows creep,
A world awakens from its sleep.
Whispers weave through twilight air,
Promises linger, soft and rare.

Beneath the veil of misty night,
Visions dance in soft moonlight.
Hands reach out to catch the glow,
Mysteries hidden, yet to show.

Dreamers wander, lost in thought,
In fields of wonder, battles fought.
Each heartbeat echoes, strong and true,
A symphony known by but a few.

As stars unveil their distant tales,
The heart takes flight, where hope prevails.
Awake, asleep, it matters not,
For in this realm, they find their spot.

Beneath the veil, the dreams collide,
A tapestry where hopes abide.
In realms of night, they softly glide,
Together, forever, side by side.

The Forgotten Lore of the Forest

Deep in the woods where whispers dwell,
Ancient tales are cast a spell.
Roots that twist in stories old,
Mysteries wrapped in green and gold.

The trees stand tall, a solemn guard,
With secrets held, the truth is hard.
Rustling leaves in gentle sighs,
Echoes of laughter, distant cries.

In hidden glades, the shadows play,
Tracing paths where legends stay.
The owl hoots in the silver light,
A sentinel of the forest night.

Faded maps of nature's lore,
In every nook, a tale to score.
The echoes of past lives awake,
Awakening dreams that ground can shake.

Through dusk and dawn, the journey's weave,
In whispered words, we dare believe.
For in the forest's heart, we find,
The lore of ages intertwined.

Songs of the Wandering Spirits

In twilight's embrace, the spirits sing,
Songs of the past that echoes bring.
Drifting softly on the breeze,
Tales of whispers through the trees.

They wander paths of memory wide,
With every step, they will confide.
Secrets shared beneath the stars,
Stories born from ancient scars.

A flickering light guides the way,
Through haunting notes, they sway and play.
In quiet corners, they reside,
Faithful watchers, none can hide.

The melody swells, a timeless flow,
Voices rise as shadows grow.
With open hearts, we heed their call,
In songs of wanderers, we find our all.

So, when the moon paints silver trails,
And nightingale softly prevails,
Listen closely, let them steer,
For wandering spirits linger near.

The Revered Companion in Solitude

In the quiet night, I find my peace,
The stars above, in silence, cease,
A gentle breeze whispers your name,
In solitude, I'm not the same.

Your shadow dances in my mind,
A cherished bond that's hard to find,
Though miles apart, our hearts entwine,
In whispered thoughts, your light will shine.

The rustling leaves, a soothing song,
With every pulse, I feel you strong,
My revered friend, though far away,
In dreams we meet, come what may.

Through echoes of the past we tread,
On trails where once our laughter spread,
In solitude, I hold you near,
A silent oath to keep you dear.

The night unfolds with gentle grace,
In every moment, I see your face,
Though solitude may try to bind,
You'll always be my heart's true kind.

Dances of the Enchanted Willow

Beneath the shade of the willow tree,
A secret world, just you and me,
With twirling leaves, we spin and sway,
In nature's arms, we linger and play.

The whispers carried by the breeze,
A melody that brings us ease,
Dancing shadows in the glow,
Where only we two dare to go.

As twilight falls, the colors blend,
The sky ignites, the day must end,
In starlit dreams, the music flows,
While under moonlight, the spirit glows.

Together in this sacred space,
We twine like vines in soft embrace,
Time stands still, the world fades out,
In our own realm, there is no doubt.

As dawn arrives with gentle light,
The willow bends, a graceful sight,
We'll meet again, come rain or shine,
In dances shared, our souls align.

Echoes from the Ancient Hearth

In the stillness where the memories dwell,
Echoes rise like a timeless spell,
Fires burned brightly in days of yore,
Whispers of stories lost on the floor.

Through the crackling flames, shadows play,
Telling tales of a distant day,
With laughter and tears shared by all,
The warmth of the ember, a siren's call.

Gaze into the glow, remember well,
The moments captured, like a shell,
In the heart of the night, we find our roots,
The pulse of our ancestors softly shoots.

Ancient hearts beat in harmony,
Each flicker and spark, a memory,
Bound by the flame, forever linked,
In every whisper, our bonds are inked.

As the embers fade, the night draws near,
Embrace the echo, hold it dear,
For in the quiet, life carries on,
In the heart's language, we are never gone.

Lullabies of the Wandering Moon

In the silver light, the moon does weave,
Soft lullabies that whisper, believe,
A gentle tug upon the silent sea,
In dreams, magical worlds roam free.

With every phase, a story told,
In glowing hues of silver and gold,
The nightingale sings, the stars align,
As echoes of comfort in moonlight entwine.

Through shadows deep and twilight's grace,
The wandering moon finds its place,
A guardian bruising fears away,
In twilight charms, we drift and sway.

As night unfolds its velvet robe,
Each shimmer a delicate probe,
In solitude's heart, we softly swoon,
Wrapped in the lullabies of the moon.

Awake or asleep, we feel the glow,
Of ancient tales from long ago,
In the cradle of night, let dreams bloom,
Embrace the magic of the wandering moon.

Secrets of the Forgotten Forest

In shadows deep where whispers glide,
The ancient trees hold secrets wide.
Beneath their boughs, the lost paths lie,
With echoes soft, of time gone by.

The mossy stones, they softly weep,
For ancient tales their guardians keep.
A rustle here, a fleeting glance,
In twilight's glow, the spirits dance.

The winding trails in silence beckon,
To hidden dreams that time has reckoned.
A world away from human strife,
Where nature breathes, and finds its life.

In rustling leaves, the past remains,
Wrapped in mist, lost in the chains.
Of secrets held, and magic stored,
The forest breathes, forever adored.

So wander slow, with heart attuned,
Embrace the silence, let it crooned.
For every tree, a story waits,
In secrets kept, the forest sates.

The Call of the Enchanted Stream

In moonlit streams where waters sing,
A gentle call, the night does bring.
With silver gleam, the ripples play,
And dance along the shimmering way.

The whispers soft, like secrets shared,
Invite the wanderer who dared.
To seek the depths where wonders flow,
A world within, a hidden show.

Beneath the waves, a songbird's tune,
Emerges bright, beneath the moon.
In every drop, a tale unfolds,
Of dreams and wishes, bright and bold.

The banks adorned with blossoms rare,
Embrace the stream with fragrant air.
As waters weave through ancient stone,
The heart finds peace, no longer alone.

So listen close, let spirit steer,
To where the water spirits cheer.
The enchanted stream will guide your way,
With magic pure, both night and day.

Phantom Steps on Ancient Roads

Along the paths of stone and dust,
The phantom steps invite the trust.
Of those who walked in ages past,
Their shadows linger, shadows cast.

The echoes haunt, a tender thread,
Of whispers soft, of words unsaid.
In twilight's glow, you feel the sway,
Of ancient souls who lost their way.

With every stride, the ground recalls,
The stories etched within the halls.
Of fleeting dreams and battles fought,
The lessons learned, the wisdom sought.

In every bend, a specter's sigh,
A soft lament as ages fly.
They beckon you, with hearts of flame,
To join the dance, to know their name.

So tread with care, but don't despair,
For in the whispers, love is there.
The ancient roads, with spirits blessed,
Their stories weave, our souls to rest.

The Dreamweaver's Lament

In twilight's weave, the dreams unfold,
A tapestry of tales retold.
The dreamweaver sighs, a heavy heart,
For every thread, a tale must part.

With eyes aglow, the visions fade,
As nightingale sings and shadows wade.
Each dream a spark, a fleeting trace,
A moment lost in time and space.

The quiet sorrow of dreams unheard,
Of silent hopes, each whispered word.
In shadows cast, the heart does yearn,
For dreams once held, that fade and burn.

Yet in her hands, the magic flows,
A gentle touch, to heal the woes.
With every tear, a star is born,
To light the night, a new dawn's horn.

So dream again, though sorrow lingers,
Let hope ignite, with tender fingers.
For in the weave, life finds its way,
The dreamweaver smiles, come what may.

A Journey into the Heart of Whimsy

In fields of laughter, dreams take flight,
Where colors dance in the morning light.
The breeze whispers secrets, soft and sweet,
As the world awakens beneath our feet.

Each corner holds a tale untold,
In every shadow, wonders unfold.
With a sprinkle of magic, hearts take chance,
And the mind tumbles into a fanciful dance.

The sky, a canvas, ever so wide,
With clouds like creatures, they drift and glide.
Every moment, a spark of delight,
In this whimsical realm, the soul takes flight.

Through winding paths of giggles and glee,
We treasure each moment, just you and me.
In this enchanted wonderland we roam,
Our laughter echoes, we've found our home.

So let us wander, hand in hand,
In this vibrant, bedazzled land.
In the heart of whimsy, we shall stay,
Creating futures, come what may.

The Lost Chronicles of Starlight

In the midnight sky, a story lies,
Whispers of starlight, ancient sighs.
From astral seas where dreams are spun,
Chronicles awaken, a race begun.

These tales of wonder, drifting far,
Guide wandering souls like a tuning star.
Each twinkle a tale, each shimmer a song,
In the silence of night, we all belong.

With comets trailing fiery grace,
We chase the shadows, find our place.
Through cosmic whispers, we journey deep,
In the lost chronicles, our secrets keep.

Galaxies spin with stories entwined,
Of hearts that wander, lost yet aligned.
In the dark embrace, we find our light,
In the lost chronicles, we reconnect our sight.

So let us soar on wings of dreams,
Across the vast, celestial streams.
In the fabric of starlight, we shall weave,
A tapestry of wonder, for all to believe.

The Allure of the Infinite Trail

Where mountains rise and rivers flow,
An infinite trail begins to glow.
With each step, the horizon calls,
A path of wonders beneath the sprawl.

In meadows lush, with whispers profound,
Nature's symphony creates the sound.
Every footfall writes a tale,
On the allure of the infinite trail.

Through forests deep where shadows play,
We wander freely, come what may.
With every turn, new sights unfold,
Adventures waiting, treasures untold.

The sun dips low, a golden hue,
In the evening glow, we find what's true.
With hearts ablaze, we chase the sun,
On the infinite trail, we are forever one.

In the stillness, dreams take flight,
Under the stars, we dance in the night.
With every breath, we embrace the tale,
Of the journey we seek on this infinite trail.

Songs from the Edge of Eternity

At the dusk of time, a melody flows,
From the edge of eternity, where mystery grows.
Echoes of laughter, whispers of grace,
In the twilight's glow, we find our place.

With notes like starlight, softly they chime,
In the silence, we dance, lost in rhyme.
Each song a memory, a heartbeat shared,
Under the cosmos, we felt prepared.

From the depths of silence, a symphony blooms,
Illuminating shadows, dispelling the glooms.
In the heartbeat of stars, we weave our dreams,
Crafting a harmony that forever redeems.

With voices rising, we chant the lore,
Of life, of love, and all we adore.
From the edge of eternity, let us sing,
For every moment, a gift we bring.

So gather round, let the songs ignite,
As we embrace the tapestry of night.
In the glow of forever, our spirits entwine,
Singing songs from the edge, where our hearts align.

Secrets Beneath the Moonlit Canopy

Underneath the silver glow,
Whispers dance upon the breeze.
Shadows weave their stories slow,
In the arms of ancient trees.

Stars like secrets softly gleam,
Veiled in night, in hushed delight.
Every glance a fleeting dream,
Lost within the tender light.

Time stands still in hushed repose,
Nature holds its breath in awe.
Where the wildflower gently grows,
And the world feels pure and raw.

Through the branches, doubts take flight,
Finding peace in sacred night.
Every sigh a soft invite,
To the magic lost from sight.

In the silence, secrets lie,
Wrapped in moonlit mysteries.
Underneath the velvet sky,
Awakening ancient histories.

The Serpent's Embrace

In the shadows, silence waits,
With a whisper, darkness calls.
Serpents slide through woven gates,
Where the echo softly falls.

Every coil a story spun,
Wrapped in nature's sly embrace.
Fingers trace where shadows run,
In this labyrinthine space.

Beneath the scales, the heart beats,
With each rhythm, life unfolds.
In this dance where time depletes,
Ancient magic softly holds.

Wisdom lingers in the air,
Teaching whispers in the night.
Secrets given, none to share,
Lost within the dreamer's sight.

In the twilight, spirits blend,
Fading in a soft embrace.
Where the serpent knows no end,
Time and fate in tender grace.

Ethereal Footprints in Starlight

Upon the shore of endless dreams,
Footprints trace the cosmic sand.
Each step echoes silent screams,
In the vastness, lost, we stand.

Ethereal glow like silver tears,
Winding through the night so clear.
Guiding souls through ancient years,
In the light, we find no fear.

Skies adorned with scattered light,
Every star a tale retold.
In the quiet, hearts take flight,
Chasing shadows, brave and bold.

Waves of time caress our feet,
As we dance through cosmic haze.
In the stillness, life's heartbeat,
Marks the moments, fleeting days.

In the darkness, hope ignites,
Filling voids with dreams so bright.
Through the endless, starry nights,
We transcend the weight of fright.

Journey Through the Veiled Realms

Through the mist, the path unfolds,
Veiled in whispered tales of yore.
Every step a secret holds,
Leading to the unknown shore.

In the twilight, shadows blend,
Guiding souls to places rare.
Where the dreamers' visions send,
Dancing with the midnight air.

Time does bend in swirling mist,
Past and future intertwine.
Every moment, love persists,
Guided by the stars' design.

Faintly calling, echoes hum,
Lost within the ancient lore.
In the silence, hearts become,
Channels to forevermore.

Through the veils, our spirits soar,
Carrying the light we find.
Journey deep, forevermore,
In the realms of heart and mind.

9 781805 619321